A Ladybird Bible Book

In the Beginning

Text by Jenny Robertson
Illustrations by Alan Parry

Scripture Union/Ladybird

There was no world at all in the beginning: it was all empty and dark. God was there. God was not empty or dark. God made light and saw how good it was. Now life could begin!

He shaped the world, making moons and planets and stars. God made the sky, the land and the sea. The world was warm. Fire rumbled in the heart of great mountains. They exploded. The hot earth cooled, leaving rich soil where plants could grow. God was pleased with the world he formed.

God wanted things to grow on earth. Green shoots sprang up in the good soil, and flowers opened gay petals. Grass spread over the land and trees gave pleasant shade. Their leaves rustled in the wind that blew gently over God's bright world.

The green shoots grew tall and yellow. Grain ripened in the sun, but no little harvest mice ran through the corn. No birds nested in the tall trees. No children played yet in the new world.

So God spoke to the sea and the sky: 'Be filled with living things, too!'

God filled the sea with fish of every shape and colour. In the sky above birds flew, soaring high as they sang their songs. Large animals roamed over the earth. Insects and creeping things crawled.

God blessed them. Their numbers grew. God was pleased with everything he made.

The earth was ready for people to live in it. God took a handful of soil and made man and breathed life-giving breath into him. He was different from the animals and other living things. The man opened his eyes and looked with wonder at God's world. 'I have made you like myself,' said God. 'You have a mind: You can understand how beautiful the world about you is. You can love. You can speak.

'All this new world is for you. I have given
you all you need. You can grind corn to make
flour for your bread. You can pick fruit. It is
good to eat and keeps you well. Water, which
makes the crops grow as it flows over the land,
is good for you to drink. Use this new world
well.'

God placed man in a beautiful garden called
Eden. The man wandered alone in the garden.
He used his eyes and saw flowers so beautiful
that he stretched out his hands to touch them.
Sounds came to his ears: the glad songs of
many birds, and the sound of running water.
He caught the water in his cupped hands. He
felt hungry. Using his tongue he tasted sweet
fruit. Everything was good.

The man was happy in the beautiful garden. Best of all, God spoke to him.

God said: 'Look after my garden. Eat as much fruit as you like from any of the trees, but in the middle of the garden grows one tree whose fruit you must not eat. This fruit would make you understand everything, bad things as well as good. You will die the day you eat this fruit.'

'It is not good for the man to be alone,' God said. 'Let the animals keep him company.'

God brought the animals and the birds to the man, and the man gave them their names. He named the lumbering elephant from the plains and the swift deer from the hills. He named the spider and the ladybird, the eagle and the sparrow. The woolly, new-born lamb frisked between the huge paws of a strong, powerful beast, to whom the man gave the name: 'lion'.

Delightedly the man played with his new friends until he began to feel drowsy. He lay down and fell asleep.

'Although the animals can help the man and he can play with them, he is still alone in Eden,' thought God. While the man slept deeply, God made a woman. He brought her to the man who looked up in delight.

'Now I am truly happy. You have given me the partner I need and I am complete!' the man exclaimed joyfully.

'She is your wife. She is the other part of human kind,' God replied.

The man held out his hand to his wife. Together they wandered through the garden. They wore no clothes, but it did not matter to them. Whatever they needed to eat or drink they found around them in the garden God gave them.

The man and his wife spent happy days in the
garden. They tilled the soil and planted seeds.
They pruned the trees, breaking off boughs so
that others might grow more thickly. They
picked fruit. The animals often helped, and in
their turn they cared for the animals and the
birds. Whenever they felt tired they rested in the
shade. Whenever they felt hungry they ate. In
the evenings, when the garden was quiet and
cool, the Lord God walked among the trees.

Whenever he called them they both ran to him, drawn by the sound of his voice.

The man and the woman loved each other, and never spoke angrily or quarrelled.

One day the woman wandered on her own
until she came to a beautiful tree she had never
seen before. Its branches were bowed beneath
the weight of shining fruit which looked so
delicious the woman longed to taste some.

As she looked longingly at the fruit she heard
a rustle among the leaves. A long snake was
coiled around the trunk. Now the snake was the
most cunning creature of all, and, to the
woman's surprise, it began to question her.

'Did God really tell you not to eat any fruit at
all from the trees in the garden?'

'Not at all!' the woman answered. 'We may eat as much fruit as we like, except from one tree. God warned us that we should die the day we eat its fruit.'

'Surely God hasn't said so?' hissed the snake. 'See, you have found this delicious fruit God spoke of: the fruit that makes you understand everything. Eat. You will become wise.'

'How wonderful to be wise!' sighed the woman, tricked by the snake. 'Besides, that fruit looks so sweet and juicy. I shall taste some!' She picked the fruit and ate it slowly. Then she heard her husband coming.

'I have found the sweetest fruit in the garden,' she called.

'You have eaten the fruit we mustn't taste!' the man exclaimed in dismay. 'God said we should die the day we eat this fruit.'

'I have eaten and have not died!' she laughed. 'The fruit has given me wisdom, and I know everything.'

'Give me this fruit! I'll have some and become wise, too,' said the man.

He ate the fruit. At once they looked at each other with their new understanding.

'We are naked!' they realised, and now they felt ashamed, so they tore down thick leaves from the fig tree and sewed them together to make clothing.

That evening they heard the Lord God as he walked in his garden, and they felt a new thing: fear. They had broken the only rule in the garden, and they hid, afraid.

'Where are you?' God called. The man and the woman crept out to meet him, but their friendship with God was spoilt.

'I was afraid because I was naked, and so I hid,' the man lied.

'How did you know you were naked?' God asked. 'Did you pick the fruit I said you were not to eat?'

'It was the woman,' he blamed his wife. 'She ate first.'

'Why did you eat the fruit?' God asked.

'The snake persuaded me,' she answered.

'Evil has come into the garden,' said God. 'Do you hear, snake? From now on this woman's children are your enemies, and you shall always crawl along the ground.'

Then God told the woman: 'Because you did what the snake told you, you will give birth to your babies in pain, and know longing and sorrow in your marriage.'

'You, man, had an easy life here. The ground gave you good crops which you harvested with ease. From now on you will sweat for your food.'

Then God made clothing out of animal skins. He clothed the man and the woman, and then he sent them away from Eden for ever. Sadly, they wandered away from the garden. One day their bodies would die, but death had come to them already. All the fresh loveliness they knew in God's perfect garden withered the day they disobeyed God's rule and ate the fruit that would make them wise.

Glory to God!

PRAISE the Lord, my soul!
O Lord, my God, how great you are! . . .
You make springs flow in the valleys,
and rivers run between the hills.
They provide water for the wild animals;
there the wild donkeys quench their thirst.
In the trees near by,
the birds make their nests and sing.

When Adam and Eve spoiled God's new world
by disobeying him it looked as though everything had gone wrong. People's lives were filled
with sadness and pain, they lied and cheated and
robbed and murdered each other.

But, although things were so different, God
still cared about the world he had made. He still
spoke to men and women and boys and girls,
and some listened to him, and became his
friends. When people looked around them there
was still beauty and wonder to be found in the
things God had made. They wanted to praise
God for the world they saw. The words at the
top of the page are part of a song written by one
of God's friends, David, thousands of years
ago. You can find it in the Bible in Psalm 104.

We can see God's work in the world today.
Trees and flowers, clouds and stars all remind us
of him because he made them. Count how many
things you can see around you which are part of
God's creation. You might like to write your
own song to thank God for them.